Hanoi
Seoul
Poems

국립중앙도서관 출판시도서목록(CIP)

Hanoi-Seoul poems / by Kim Jung Hwan.
— Seoul : Munhakdongne, 2003
 p. ;   cm

ISBN 89-8281-712-3 02810 : ₩6500

811.6-KDC4
895.715-DDC21   CIP2003000898

Kim Jung Hwan

Hanoi
Seoul
Poems

munhakdongne

Hanoi-Seoul Poems

by Kim Jung Hwan

Copyright © Kim Jung Hwan 2003
All rights reserved.
MUNHAKDONGNE Publishing Co., Ltd, Seoul

6F, Dongsomun B/D, 260 Dongsomundong 4ga,
Seongbukku, Seoul, 136-034, Korea
phone 82-2-927-6790~5, 927-6751~2
fax 82-2-927-6753
editor@munhak.com
www.munhak.com

The openning of new millennium brought me to Hanoi, Vietnam. Stay was short but, soon, as if in Seoul, life became familiar, familiarity wondrous. And, wonder continues It is one and half year since departure from Hanoi, and, in half-millennium old and commonplace Seoul, Hanoi is familiar and wondrous by chance. 「Hanoi-Seoul poems」 are dedicated to Vietnamese writers who welcomed us with warmth, poet Huu Thinh, Du At, and novelist Bao Ninh among them. May 'sorrows of war' grow into, joy of liberation and peace.

Aug. 2003

Kim Jung Hwan

Contents

Midwinter
—Hanoi–Seoul poems : prelude

Walking the sleet falling road walking

Façade rich but 1970's

Of economic development without Park-Chung-Hee.*

Road of sordid back street walking

Underground draft beer-house smelling worn, rainy summer

Boiled eggs' hole-small store and singer-drinker room's

Straggling neon-signs are rejuvenescing walking road between

Low-stature naked household dwellings and service-category business livelihood

Walking humid road between sleet falling

Reminiscences are lecherous,

Yes. Walking Pyongyang road without Kim-Il-

Sung** also.

10

Airport
—Hanoi–Seoul poems 1

One hundred-years' war is at ease at Hanoi airport

Before formalities for entry already the starred army
badge of rank

Uniformed public safety officer looks emaciated as
at country side

Tour suitcases resembling homecoming bundles

A station building that barely evaded air raids

Is more at ease than ruined clock.

I have a flash of memory that $5 \cdot 16^*$ to no purpose
distinguishes

Major general Park-Chung-Hee's jet-black Ray Ban.

Only coup d'etats are spiteful and disjointed.

One hundred year's war is at ease one hundred
year's war that winned the day against imperial-
lism(this word already sounds clamorous)

Is mild dignity

That holds back apologies.

This sounds clamorous, too.

$6 \cdot 25^{**}$ & $4 \cdot 19^{***}$, and $5 \cdot 16$.

Numbers are clamorous

Why did we make a living with our teeth so clenched.

* 1961. 5. 16. Military coup d'etat by Park-Chung-Hee.
** 1950. 6. 25. Korean Civil war.
*** 1960. 4. 19. Student revolution.

First paddy fields and dry fields
— Hanoi–Seoul poems 2

Left and right unfold paddy fields as first snow
falling
As not once not henceforth cold first snow falling
And over them meticulous uncle Ho-Chi-Min's
Standing signboard passes like poor days'
Beautiful future visions.
Yes. Really. Seems like 60's without Park-Chung-
Hee or
70's without anti-communist education. As shabby
smelled shaven head middle-high schoolboy
Me that in the defected spies anti-communist public
lectures' south-dispatches and secret manoeuvres
Learned drama
Me that thoroughgo neither anti-communism nor
arts
Me that is relieved by the fact too late

No, New Village Movement should not be like that,

No, factory constructions, too, should not be like that,

Me that smelled erotic love's scandalous smell first

As an undergraduate fourth-grade, Me that suffered

A shock of overlapping of Vietnam's 'decline and liberation'

What is the trouble of my being again in old day's barracks

Sick of being in again but as if by fate like an old-timer in sickness

Dreaming a nightmare me.

Anyway that time and tide unfolds among trees

As first snow falling unfolds paddy fields and dry fields at an Hanoi

Outer ring road where vestiges of air raid leaves

here and there fingerprints as those of the human.

Unfolds a two-lane road where pulling-down and construction progress simultaneously.

Quite so. It is trivial, and as natural as trivial······

Time and tide unfold, of 'some kinds and duplicity'.

Downtown

— Hanoi–Seoul poems 3

'energetic commotion of liberation⋯⋯ '

Roads are narrow, and young male and female packing Japan-made autobike

Traffic congestion overflowing Hanoi downtown passing through

I said to guide-interpreter Mrs. Hoa,

'energetic commotion of liberation⋯⋯ '

What this means? Indeed, feelings come nearly but do not come again

Into a Korean translation.

Mrs. Hoa attains appearances of an corpulent version South-Korean female TV talent nearly and

Firmly the topics were Vietnam-hitting South-Korean female TV talent's fashion hot wind.

Streets seems near Cheong-Gye[*] ditch 4th, 5th street

Where material odds of blue jeans shops share

same, feel-funny because fall-behind rooms

With SONY, SAMSUNG electric home appliances
agencies.

It's the same in English-Korean dictionary. English-
speaking whiles

Make me a colonial commoner without fail. Maybe
not when reading but

At least during English conversations grammer
determines action. 'energetic commotion of libera-
tion······'

Autobikes, student lovers rushes without divisional
strips

Without U-turn prohibitions. They are most of all
transport-arbeiting students······

Mrs. Hoa enlarged upon, but

Their driving skills that are more smart than

Old day's worn-out fighter-plane's vietminh pilots

Understand not a violent temper but vitality

That generations of war should bequeath to future
peace posterity.

I have no Korean language to describe it.

Only colonial words.

energetic commotion of liberation.

power more free than freedom.

* In Seoul, means 'transparent stream'.

Madison Hotel

—Hanoi–Seoul poems 4

Wake up at daybreak to open the window

Rain falls on the slant roof beyond Madison Hotel

On the Rex Hotel roof

Rain falls slant, too.

Age of French colonialism

Is modest, not five-starred

Flashing magnificent hotel but near

Estate-class inn of privacy where grace and

Passages chop in doors, doors chop in passages
sometimes.

Last night air conditioner had gone off.

Modest is now the collusion

That enabled the french mainland-born or well-
taught interpreter

Families' better days.

The wetness is chilly but here

Is little chance of January bitter cold of Seoul.

No more chance of the rainy spell in Hanoi at January.

Shall I rain slant, too.

A short while anxious about mouths to feed, Japan's and

US' situations.

Colony is in danger.

Rain falls on the slant roof

Beyond Madison Hotel on the Rex Hotel roof

Rain falls slant.

Thing, kung, rhang, sheung, chyong, zeung······

Still I can't alphabetize Vietnamese pronunciations.

Air raids and memories

—Hanoi–Seoul poems 5

I have no memory of air raids. 6 · 25

Pictures are, history is, but too wretched

To become every day life

I am not seized with terrors of air raid, don't talk nonsense,

Thanks to my father whose memories were air-raided

Our home was peaceful

Hanoi has no memory of air raids, too.

Because too near

Pictures are, history is, memorials are, but

Air raids and parents are, nearer than that,

Life and poverty are more nearer than that

Flattened two-stories or three-stories or

Shoddy houses still in former days,

Dwelling houses on a vast empty plain, seems

bombed, seems in construction

Trio

—Hanoi-Seoul poems 6

In front of French Louis Napoleon empire-mode
National History Museum
　Where archaeological excavation materials become
national liberation movement
　Stands Mrs. Hoa like a sightseeing guide auntie
　In front of austere history's Confucius tomb
　More clear, but more ambiguous so much too, Mrs.
Hoa
　Stands like a sightseeing guide auntie

　Made for enjoyment of sunlight-glaring Hanoi's
outdoor
　But now chinese restaurant, in front of a sign-board
entrance
　Old, face black-hardened poet Du At
　With two hands folded and raised, with hearty

cheers

Greeted South-Korean writers as if greeting his comrades

Ardently, face beaming all over, he

Witnessed ardor of revolution but

Witnessed also an age of South-Korea

When revolutionary ardor fall into the wish-washy.

'Vietnamese are generous welcomers. Country's local products are plentiful, in fact······ Moreover for foreign visitors.'

Neither bright nor dark, neither gorgeous nor squalid

With a red-colored handy stage and a big eating table

In chinese restaurant, alert to abundant foodstuffs and

A beauty singer and a small band

That can play South-Korean Noraebang[*] hit songs,

Sits the president of Vietnam Writers Association
Huu Thinh,

Seems like Che Guevara

He is a veteran retired colonel. Indeed in Hanoi all

Veterans seem like Che Guevara. Not Che of Jesus in
rags

But that of virtuous fatness Buddha

He bestowed a favor of grain wine, met moi,

Rye fermentation, fairly strong, but taste of scorched
rice-tea

My nationalism does not end here.

After the 'Korean-mode' banquet Mrs. Hoa mounts a new-generation

Autobikes wears a headmask and with a poop-poop,

From out-of-the-way place into the drunkard's red-painting

Sections disappears. As it happens, I feel my shoulders shaken.

I would like to follow married she, a Vietnamese household

Sorry, rainy, beautiful day

* means 'singing-room'.

To Halong Bay

—Hanoi–Seoul poems 7

A scenic masterpiece of sea and islands,

Halong Bay is north-west Vietnam Quang Ninh.

'To arrive there we ought to pass by the sliding

sash-window red roofs and

Red river and a threadbare iron-bridge.'

Pass by dust-storm raising new-construction road,

water buffaloes several thousand miles far away,

Pass by several ten years battered, tall-height trucks,

Everywhere same same mongrels and

A good-natured foreman, uncle Ho-Chi-Min and

Similar village people and people's minds,

The tombs of the unknown soldiers in every village,

Pass by everywhere grimed smudged children we

must

'At the pressing danger of country mother dragon and child dragons

Arrive there, to stay forever defending the country.'
Beautiful

Halong Bay covers 1,553 square kilometers, island 1,969 pieces

For the people of war capital Hanoi

Beauty is destiny.

Since twenty thousand years ago aborigines living

Late paleolithic, early neolithic age,

Since Soi Nhu, Cai Beo, Ha Long

Three great culture succeed

Halong Bay, beauty is a destiny that takes only several hours

A destiny is Ho-Chi-Min Memorial Park

Where dignities of the past and future visions

Meet modestly.

Halong Bay, Beauty is history and destiny.

Halong Bay

— Hanoi–Seoul poems 8

By five dollars per head

We engaged a whole four-hour Halong Bay tour
boat

Lunch was abundant with steamed flower-crabs
and hard-boiled shrimps,

Jade green waters are at ease embracing islands

Islands, left and right or before my eyes

Rise approaching like a monstrous giant surprising
the prow but

Nearer, island's root wearing

Pains embracing,

Raging waves are so much

At ease too, on the sea islands, between islands

Sea-roads are vast and beautiful and

The more vast, the more beautiful and

At last fatigued life unfolds so much beautiful

30

Lifetime of ordinariness

O, tolérance

Sea-depths are invisible

Terribleness have no smell and taste

On the lapping surfaces conch trumpet shell

The single-oar powerboats selling marine products
are busy

'Only a unmoved father who moves a boat

And a child, with two fragile arms raised in

Purchase begging. Is a mother at home?······ No,

Perhaps dead. In respect of war.'

The sea, on her way to beauty and sorrow

Arrives in the end at road

Where sorrows are so much sufficient

Thien Cung Grotto

A limestone cave shellfish shells heaped. 'Here

A piracy suits us down to the ground.'

'As you likes it? Real committing needs half pirates,

Half hostages. So it brings in ransom······'

Tour boat deck laps, too shallow

Upon Hanoi's breast Halong Bay laps

'How regrettable French guys should be to yield
here.'

'Why, beautiful of course. People say it in 1994
registered into UNESCO World Nature Heritages.'

Again, to Hanoi

—Hanoi–Seoul poems 9

Returning roads are Halong Bay, tears gather

Loaded into a worn-out ten-men vehicle

Returning roads are Halong Bay, in a Korean mode,

Like a rural lucid scene

Where rain makes the forest more black the lakes
more bright

Outside the window earlier darkness spreads and

In the outer-ring villages of electric power shortage

Besides we can see sight of the night

Descending in embracement of something

Hanoi nearer, more homesick

Though in Hanoi we will not be able to

Go further than a little soggy 1970's outskirts of Shin-
Chon*

That may not be called a homecoming

Then why, homesick?

It is a road that I could not take.

A road without terror

War ends and at length people's

Villages embrace a night as mouths to feed.

Ah, this, tranquilities and pieties

Returning roads are Halong Bay, tears gather

* In Seoul, means 'new village'.

Van Nghe newspaper company

—Hanoi–Seoul poems 10

'You see Vietnamese likes poems.'

Collections of poems may sell better in Vietnam but

That wordings of editor-in-chief of

One hundred thousand copies publishing Van Nghe

newspaper company to me

Sounds ill omen

'It's age of Kim-So-Wol[*], still far to go.'

So much my mind that writes poetry in South-Korea

Is a defeatist over 70 years

I see all, soon come ages of film and TV mass-

culture, and

Multimedia, indeed those have come. Poetry

In Vietnam greets the more

premodern age

'If selected in early January collection the poet
receives contribution fee amounting six-month's
salary.'

Can poetry penetrate through capitalism?
Penetrating poetry loses the masses and not to lose
Poetry cannot help desperately relying on the
premodern
Can poetry overcome this bitter sorrow?

O, bitter sorrow. Yes. In Vietnam, Hanoi,
Japanese & Chinese mode and Korean mode, though
superficial in all,
Is less superficial than bitter sorrow

Is there a way of poetry

For stature of sorrow to get over sorrow's wretched-
ness,

Is there a road of poetry

So to take off, correct

This age of the postmodern when circulation ex-
ploits production and

Forms suppress contents?

Van Nghe newspaper company

Where socialist dignities of literature mingle in a
long-standing mother-of-pearl cabinet

With 1950's atmosphere of Cheong-Eum^{**} publish-
er's editorial department

When literature and publishing was hope 6 · 25

before and after,

    Spreading giddy outside the window

    Crowded red-painting, resembling Seoul poorly,

    A look of the night view of Hanoi asked so

    So much my defeatism drifted away

* A Korean popular poet(1902~1934).
** means 'right sound'.

Generations and family

—Hanoi–Seoul poems 11

Near ninety years old novelist Thun Qua Rheng,
who was active as a famous writer before taking up a
rifle in lieu of a pen against Japanese imperialism, so
become first generation of Vietnamese literature.
Seems like meeting again my maternal grandfather
died just 30 years before. A pointed bamboo pole a
thunderbolt from the blue establishing Mapo* dried
fishes business but boundlessly meticulous to
grandsons. Seems like that grandfather become in the
world beyond 30 years more wealthy and magnani-
mous······

At a jump over seventy years old woman essayist
Quan Rhang Ye, who was in spotlight as an expec-
tancy before taking up a rifle in lieu of a pen against
French imperialism, so become second generation of

Vietnamese literature. Seemed like meeting again my
maternal grandmother died 20 years before at the just
same age. The same features of then, when she died
as a last court lady who had married a quick-tempered
husband and still retained lifelong endurance's
benevolent wrinkles and skins that show through the
other side, one thousand years' smile, as if death is but
stoppage, but lack of color, odorless, having no
further meanings.

   This mixing up does not bring confusions, is
opulent
   And corporal clear.
   Such is history, too and families too.

   Ah, what on earth, how much, to what degree have

they fighted······ so that could become more ordinary than every day life.

After long time, at ease with timidity.

Expecting seventy years old poet Tsrui Zong is third generation of Vietnamese literature againt American imperialism. He is a nose-red alcoholic even in the official conference table. Fairly well takes too much, pent-up resentments seems visible. Seems like at South-Korean National Writer's Association, at a quarrel while drinking······ this, illusions are, why?

Just over forty years old Thang Shang Long is a many-talented versatile new, fourth generation.

Are names correct?

Still I can't alphabetize Vietnamese pronunciations.

Not hallucinations.

Pronunciations are clear as a heavy life in cheers and jumping joys.

* In Seoul, means 'hemp harbor'.

A Bao Ninh household
—Hanoi–Seoul poems 12

Hard to understand because too impeccable

Broad daylight In-Sa-Dong* taverns side street at an entrance

As before partisan-bearded Bao Ninh stands, as he did in Seoul

He is a world-renowned writer and I'm minor poet even in South-Korea but,

He is the same with me in drinking more than enough alcohols at night and

Having too much saneness in the daytime

(And seeing that way makes him resemble Cheon-In-Kwon** also)

He is a survivor from the legendary combat unit

And my situation was to patch up three years military service as an act-the-fool incompetent but

In drunkeness he and me too cannot lot out neither

Vietnam nor South-Korea.

'Spotted' more or less by Vietnamese socialist government,

But of the wealthy classes by virtue of not a little royalties and Vietnamese low prices,

He has a narrow and high, five-storied belfry house,

The ground-floor of which serves visitors second floor his pretty wife

Third floor his son fourth floor his mother inhabits. Indeed mother is

Nailed like history beautiful as permanent, and

Fifth floor, at his writing room after spreading eight or nine sorts of foodstuffs involving banh chung or bahn tet,

A perfect square amount's about 50 men portion and after setting our party eight or nine members

Down around the square thick and thick,

As if relieved now

He for the first time begins to covet derangement

He that came close to being a lost child at airport
owing to time crisscrossing

Said he hates Shin-Chon taverns side street
resembling Saigon

'Hanoi is fine, to me, though even foods are some
political.'

......

Not a little drunken, but as it was lunch, likewise

Hard to understand because too impeccable

Broad daylight In-Sa-Dong taverns side street at an
entrance

Bao Ninh stands, yes, as he did in seeing off.

Anyone who are of little use in South-Korea, if females the better.

Stay here, live together with me, he said.

Is there not any gentleman to let me go with to South-Korea,

Said his pretty wife

A vehicle laden with our party slipped out of the In-Sa-Dong side street

And entered Hanoi. Ah, Hanoi

Is more familiar than In-Sa-Dong, that fact is a long time since, and natural

* In Seoul, means 'kind-hearted temple'.
** Famous South-Korean rock singer.

People's committee

—Hanoi–Seoul poems 13

Bac Ninh People's Committee's

Vice-president is a woman

'As Mr. President suddenly happened to······'

She said, but deserved male president

Expecting becomes suddenly undeserved and

Deserved me ashamed and undeserved me

In no time natural, even admirable

Indeed, undeserved me deserved me repenting so,

Bac Ninh People's Committee for certain have

A thing that pokes smart the depth of my anti-communist drama's heart

She is a doctor of medicine. Enjoyed popularity as a spirited maiden physician and

Took up a rifle and ran into the national liberation front. Deserved.

She distinguished herself radiant. Deserved.

She is in her early forties, the goal of war didn't
damage but suitably tempered her beauty. Deserved

The accomplished is all deserved, that's right

More stirring is 'drive back' than 'triumph'

To the last. So,

Development invest-inducing project map of

Bac Ninh she briefs with a pilot pole

Is surfeited but also

Pokes the depths of 1970's that I know

'Vietnamese foodstuffs as time goes by are to my
appetite. Yet

This fish is, a carp, or catfish?'

Do not call in question

Bet either Vietnamese carp, or Vietnamese catfish.

In Vietnam, Hanoi and arounds

Are all things optimistic and, it is world's original.

Though 'world's original' as-ifs me, again, in a ward office of Republic of Korea.

Quan ho Bac Ninh

—Hanoi–Seoul poems 14

Quan ho means a shout of joy. Bac Ninh province peasants'

Traditional ballads. Sacred songs of male-female sexual delights

Arts Theatre is a international sight. Sometimes when public performances do not keep on

A special performance for foreign delegates takes place,

More artists entertaining less spectators

That day was the ease too 'Quan ho is a shout of joy. Each time a team finish their part please put a bouquet in each performer's breast.'

Performances were wonderful. An over-eighty-year-old female singer's voice

Not rusty, nor hazy,

As the vibrations of three hudred years' Vietnamese

peasants were more glaring than coloratura,

A sorrow without rhyme or reason achieved again the sorrow's stature

Vietnamese fiddle, clarinet, a large drum(female), harp, mixed with a guitar,

Exotic obvious but also as if hearing Korean classics

In which 'people' is more pompous

Male and female by turns entertaining Quan ho

Relaxed a while doing real Korean ballads but

At a drinking song of an slim and trim,

TV talent-outshining female singer-dancer

That seduced with one arm's fan stroking other arm's sleeve protractedly

Repeating submissions over and over again

Achieved sad, feudal climax of male-female sexual delights

That day's top bouquet fell into her hand.

'I see, we've been received as guests of the nation.'

Yet, why the exiting singer's figures from behind are

so

Somewhat aching, the more so because have

nothing to do with stirring?

Alas, Vietnam Folk Arts Theatre's old Quan ho

singers

Dwell in a numbered shabby room

Attached to a worn-out dresser and handy zipper-

wardrobe

Through the 1960's cement washstand gutters flow

the urines and slops together.

This scene of

A caller-waiting is, alas, sad, Hanoi, Hanoi

Your name sounds sad too.

Ly Bat De Temple

— Hanoi–Seoul poems 15

Ly Bat De means 'eight Ly-family kings.'

In 1010, Ly-Kong-Won from Koryo leaves the Korean Peninsula

He by sea, I by air arrived here.

Ly-Kong-Won entitled himself Ly Thai To, meaning 'the first king of Ly-dynasty'.

Vietnamese Ly-dynasty continued until the eighth king

To perish in 1225. Korean Ly-dynasy, starting 1392, and

To my sight perished during 1592~1598 Korea-Japan War but otherwise

Not ended yet. The matter is not the history's

But present chaos, and that the several hundred years' breadth makes

Stubborn, awefully worn-out Ly Bat De Temple's

Stupendous, cracked statuettes

Familiar like today

Statuettes obviously testify today's mysteries and hard-to-understands

Testify some kind of black holes and black hole's

Some kind of orders too

'Not Ly of plum family, as in Korea, but flower-mountain family Ly'.

Ly Bat De Temple was built in ensuing Tran-dynasty's early period

To consecrate 'Ly-family kings'

That is strange, too 'Not deafted, but downfall, maybe.'

History of downfall not defeated, was, is. 'At festivals

Eight Ly-family kings' statuettes are

Moved to Cho Phap Tower,

Where Li-Kong-Won was an acolyte.'

Ritual and, game is a good fair. Strangely, not strange.

Indeed, not strangely, strange. Chess game 'glorifying

Heroic deeds⋯⋯' is sublime. A winner in solemn

Parade turns round the temple three times

To devote thanks to gods

Goodness, the shadow of a shade. When all is said and done, travelling is too much to me⋯⋯

Time to return to my country, too

Summit talks & signature, and

—Hanoi–Seoul poems 16

Yesterday roomates poet Ko-Hyeong-Yol and novelist

Choi-In-Sok were in a severe battle blaming air-conditioner troubles upon

Each other, two men a representative each in his genre if

Best nice guy contest happens, how could they be so severe in so trivial matter, interesting to excess, said novelist Kim-In-Sook

As a best-time-missing flower, giggled and guffawed, abdomen seized and feet stumped

And today a summit talks and an agreement
Signing ceremonies are planned
Formalities are expected to be a socialist large scale.

Lee-Mun-Ku is a rising nation's, or electronic industry's novelist of agrarian literature

Who scarcely becomes formal ceremonies,

Full of knowledge and discontent, a country person of copious temper. Huu Thinh

Devoted his youth to guerilla warfare his manhood to construction of socialism

And is a poet in whose works the struggle and construction fertilize each other suitably

Lee-Mun-Ku said as a '6 · 25 son of reds' in South-Korea proper

Job to survive was a novelist and

Huu Thinh's career was of course checkered too but

Huu Thinh's checkeredness will not be able to understand

Lee-Mun-Ku's checkeredness. Even Reading his novels

Helps little.

Beyond the destiny of a minor power people and poet/novelist

Huu Thinh was forced into a war's wretchedness and furies

Lee-Mun-Ku was forced into terrible childhood memories and lifelong bare livelihood

That two men are having a summit talks. Huu Thinh is concerned

More about the Vietnam's future than South-Korea's past. Deserved.

Lee-Mun-Ku's concerns are Vietnam's spirit of tolerance

Different from North-Korea. Yes. Vietnam war is unprecedented in

Cruelties committed by U.S. Army, South-Korean soldiers included, but

More unprecedented is the tolerance

That winner to loser, warriors to betrayers showed.

As a war became a habit, maybe tolerance became a habit too,

And about by this points, maybe they understand each other not?

Lee-Mun-Ku would embrace, and Huu Thinh more hurried to

Look forward to but

About by this points maybe they recognize each other not?

Signing ceremonies opened with Ho-Chi-Min portrait
hanging red wall for backdrop,

All the representatives of Vietnam literature four
generations present at Writers Associations

Great Conference Hall, a large scale as expected

At a long table on which both nations' national flags
crisscrossed

Lee-Mun-Ku and Huu Thinh signed joint-agree-
ments.

Like some Parker fountain-pen

Like Kennedy or Nixon and red

Like socialism, not Brezhnev a little more

Like Mao Tze Tung.

Strange. Vietnam secured Soviet Union's aids and

With Red China warred for a while······

In Soviet-collapsed Russia are witnessed

Often Vietnamese students rainkicked and blowed

For being from a minor nation Soviet Russia helped

to Russia's own gourd-dipper begging

Maybe that weighed on my mind, at the lunch

banquet arranged by South-Korean part

I encouraged bomb-liquors one cup per head to

Vietnamese writers

'At South-Korea U.S. Army guys are stationed, but

this one is worth a test

All the others are of no help.'

Some sorry for agreement contexts. Manifestation of

not our apologies but mutual

Regrets. 'We have regrets that between South-Korea

and Vietnam, after both suffering the colonialist

Opression, existed once hostilities. We oppose any hostilities henceforth possible between two nations······ '

Maybe that some weighed? 'See, we are not the government. And old members of Writers Association mostly had opposed the dispatch of troops to Vietnam.' so much equivocating, maybe that some weighed?

Lost at ease : morning

—Hanoi–Seoul poems 17

Dressed off the ceremonies and starting into the
streets I am Hanoi citizen features

And the exterior seems like Vietnamese people too.
No one

Not any of cyclos and woman vendors in second-
hand aosai

Touts me. Low chairs busy taking the edge off
morning appetites in

Con Po, tire-pump store is more slack than that

Pumps are rather thrown out without knowing why

Gamblers are maybe due to socialism more at ease
than bloodshot eyes

A steamed chicken house more busy at night is not
open yet

A children-packed market-lane classroom seems

As if an air-raid shelter dug out in the someone's

childhood memories. No,

More taste of hard-headedness. Taking the edges off
appetites······ Fish pot-stew strong

With orange peel-taste spices peculiar to Vietnamese
foodstuffs now

Even appetites me. Cabs remodelled from

Imported Korea-made Pride looks older than export
and

Dong money that exchanges for not more than 1/10
won

Seems the currency reform of yesterday

No. Indeed, this simile is insufficient.

The prices are not more than 1/10 of South-Korea

So ten-thousand dongs' power reaches ten-thousand
wons.

Yes. Not only histories are compared too late

But we come to see a yesterday's today

Not today of tomorrow

Not trodden roads neither roads to go but into duplication of both

For the first time road opens and I am lost at ease into it

'Numbers on each house are too big. Rather like accommodation.'

That words missing out behind, lost

Lost at ease : night

—Hanoi–Seoul poems 18

I heard Seoul is in much more than normal

Bitter cold yet last day before departure

Having enough of Hanoi night is so humid heaty

On creaking, not unnailed chairs

We drinked with Bao Ninh without any handsome
eatables

Over one hundred cans of beer. Vietnamese product

Tiger Beer is meek. Sorrows of war warrior

Bao Ninh is this time bowed down at parting.

His son-interpreter choosed economics becoming

A new generation, and I joked, done well, novel-
writings

Surely cannot cover your father's liquor expenses
and then I

Become bowed down too. Days of son's success
indeed ought to

Make father's novelist job poor, that idea

Impends without a countermeasure. Like travels
started away unprepared

Night lose a sense of direction and so humid heaty
and even after Bao Ninh

Exited as one of remnants a good while

We have meek alcohols and not more than 1/10
prices and more low-priced

Nightscapes of Hanoi, the sorrows of unknown
nationality

Enjoyed, or lost? Dawn, two o'clock, without curfew
but

Human traces disappear as if in smallish illusive
cinema studio set and

Cyclos among themselves have good command of
Vietnamese language that sounds like passwords,

'Where is the route to Madison-Rex Hotel?' At a
moderate estimate

Less than two stations cutting out a third-rate

Ragpicker semblance saying '(S)moke, marijuana?' is
only brutal but not much threat(I got drunk?)

I walked, indomitable, at ease, lost

An address

— Hanoi–Seoul poems 19

Departure morning

Arrived at last by Ho-Chi-Min Tomb

Where meeting between past's dignities and future visions

Meet again death's solemn ordinariness

At a minority races' handwoven textile souvenir shop Hai Linh,

Madame of which have her border area noble-woman's features modest-sunburned

See, an address completes a verse

27 Ong Ich Khiem tel 04)7 · 331555

8R. Nguyen Thai Son 3 Precinct-Go Vap Dist., Ho Chi Minh City

Tel 08)8 · 955742-09160 1136

High in the air

—Hanoi–Seoul poems 20

At the time the airplane leaving Seoul were soon to arrive at Hanoi under outside window clouds

A dangerous map became easy mountains and Milky Way

River smelling human and warm-hearted

Villages, that sight made a hundred years' anti-imperialism war

Unbelievable······Victory all the more······

So it was then yet airplane is leaving Hanoi. Two p.m.

Traditional bamboo-leaf lunches Du At packed are staunch but 'Customs entry

Possible? I mean, can't let quarantined.' A lunch package is a lunch package but I, grudging the word 'political', dare not to crack and eat and

Piling it's hand and foot deep in my knapsack am

no other than a smuggler.

Yet by now maybe you

Know. Warm-hearted villages becoming easy

mountains and human-smelling

Tender river a dangerous map

On taking-off high in the air,

'Warm-hearted' aches so smart 'tender'

Sorrows so bitter you know.

......

No roads on clouds and

Clouds under so soon Seoul's

Nightscapes are gorgeous like a jewelry bouquet

and

'Gorgeous'

Sins so cruel you know.

Again, airport

—Hanoi-Seoul poems : epilogue

In early autumn outfits Kim-Po Airport is too cold
like a hungry boxer's

Punch penetrating my whole body

Cannot accuse cooking-pot-boiling superficialities, I,
either

Who in Hanoi

Begrudged ten thousand wons as if hundred thou-
sands and too cold

Takes a model taxi which takes over fifteen
thousands to return home to Dang-San-Dong.

I see why Du At packed me a lunch, cracking the

Smuggled lunch serves fine minced pork and
cooked rice

To my appetite like a rice cake

Mouths to feed agree with me too

Good-by Hanoi, seek and hide in my body tight

Peace of Sound*

— After Hanoi–Seoul poems

This is my land.

Ears

Of golden corns

That was my ears

That was rubbed by wind-sound.

Wind,

Sound is my soul

Is shudder that makes

Stillness stillness

Incense is evening dress of sound

But Mae-Hyang-Ree,**

Village that cherishes incense

Here Sound is

Decibel that tear eardrums to pieces

That fly lower than our waist

To tear whole body of drums to pieces,

Decibel of American air-forces F-16's dogs and cat's
machine gun

Bomb of Vietnam or South-America

Bomb of KwangJu, my land

You hear bomb-sound

Of terror longer than life-time

You see broken bomb-shell

Of size bigger than life-body

World of sound makig itself to inferno of devil-
torture

This is Mae-Hyang-Ree, my land

Hear Sound, flesh of sound that is torn to pieces,

Hear Sound.

But my word is my world

I say,

My world is my word

I say

See here, that rising tatter of iron

Rise up, the fallen

See here, that tatter of iron raising arts of sound

Radiating wide and wider peace of sound

Condensing boundless decibels and boundless

terror and boundless tears of tears

Rise up, O Sound

My deep-shaken, shuddering, beautiful sound of
peace

   Till sound become music

   Music become peace

   Eardrum become the native place of music.

* This poem was recited during dedication of a painter Lim-Ok-
Sang's Mae-Hyang-Ree statue <Goddess of Liberty in Korea> at
2000. 10. 20. Olympic Park anti-ASEM mass demonstration, in
Korean and English, by turns.
** means 'the village that cherishes incense'.